HAL LEONARD GUITAR METHOD BOOK 3

BY WILL SCHMID AND GREG KOCH

T0045536

ISBN 978-0-7935-1156-3

HAL•LEONARD® CORPORATION

7777 W. BLUEMOUND RD. P.O. BOX 13819 MILWAUKEE, WI 53213

Visit Hal Leonard Online at
www.halleonard.com

THE MAJOR SCALE

A **scale** is a series of notes arranged in a specific order. Perhaps the most common scale is the **major scale**. It is used as the basis for countless melodies, riffs, solos, and chord progressions.

Scales are constructed using a combination of whole steps and half steps. (Remember: on the guitar, a half step is the distance of one fret; a whole step is two frets.) All major scales are built from the following step pattern.

WHOLE – WHOLE – HALF – WHOLE – WHOLE – WHOLE – HALF

This series of whole and half steps gives the major scale its characteristic sound.

C MAJOR SCALE

To build a C major scale, start with the note C and follow the step pattern from above.

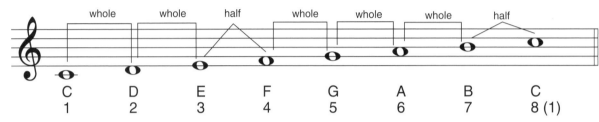

The first (and eighth) degree of a major scale is called the keynote or **tonic**. This is the "home" tone on which most melodies end.

Practice the C major scale ascending and descending in first position.

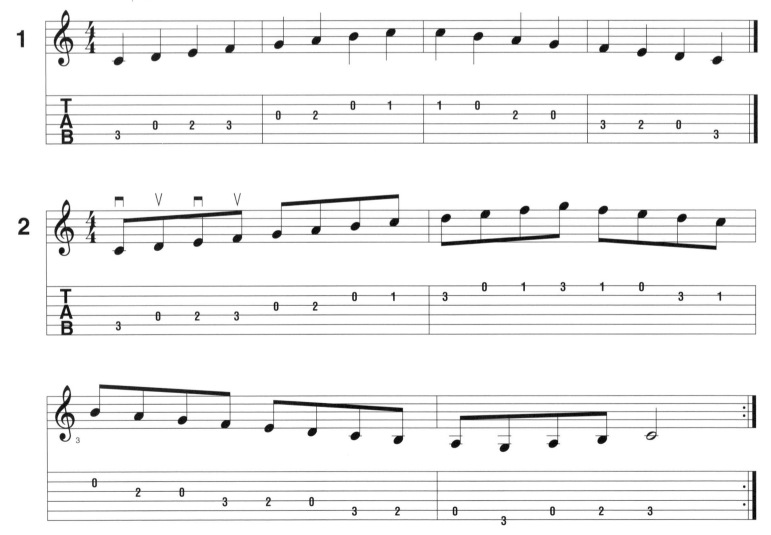

Try this: start on second string, first fret C and play a major scale up the second string using the pattern of whole and half steps.

Chords and chord progressions are also derived from scales. A piece of music based on the C major scale is in the key of C major. For every key, there are seven corresponding chords—one built on each note of the major scale.

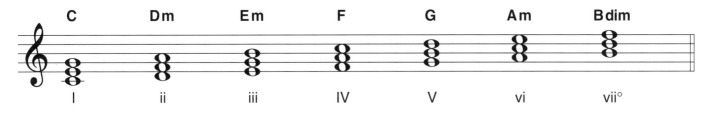

Note: Triads (three-note chords) use every other note of a scale (1-3-5, 2-4-6, etc.). Roman numerals are used to label a chord's location within a key.

By taking a closer look at each of the seven chords, notice that major triads are built on the first, fourth, and fifth notes of the scale; minor triads are built on the second, third, and sixth notes of the scale; and a diminished triad is built on the seventh note of the scale. The seven chords are common to the key of C because all seven contain only the notes of the C major scale (no sharps or flats). It is important to memorize this sequence of chord types, as it applies to all major scales.

The following examples are in the key of C. Practice playing the chords; then try improvising using the C major scale. When beginning to improvise, play the scale ascending and descending and notice how the notes work over the chords. Then, mix up the notes. It helps to emphasize the chord tones.

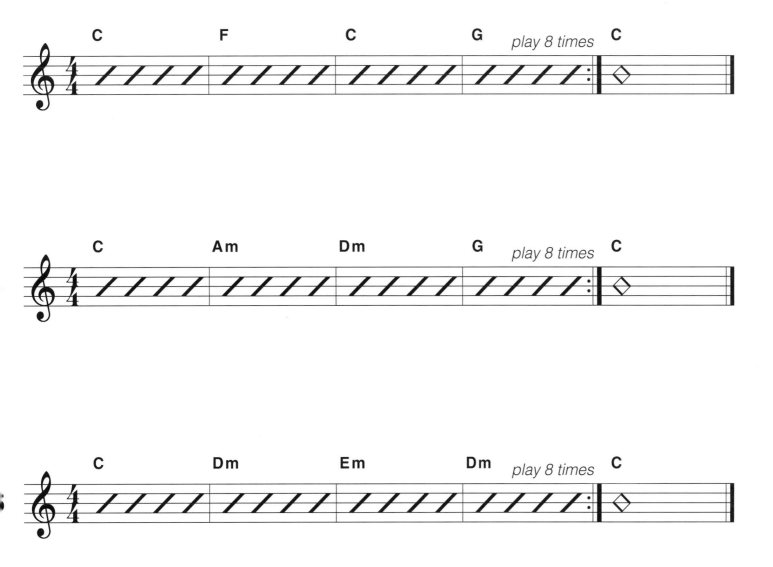

See the Reference Section at the end of this book for more information on chord construction.

G MAJOR SCALE

To build a G major scale, start with the note G and apply the major-scale step pattern. The F is sharped to complete the pattern.

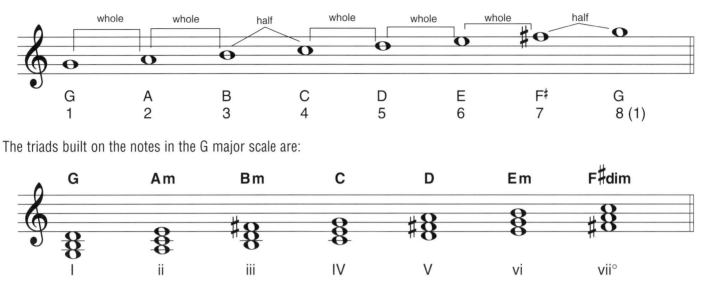

The triads built on the notes in the G major scale are:

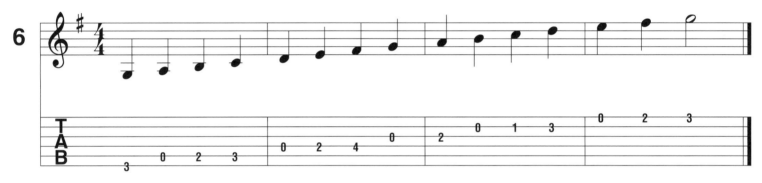

Practice the G major scale in first position. Remember: the key signature for G major is one sharp (F#).

Now play a well-known melody using notes and chord from the G major scale.

THE FIRST NOEL

D MAJOR SCALE

To build a D major scale, start with the note D and apply the major-scale step pattern.

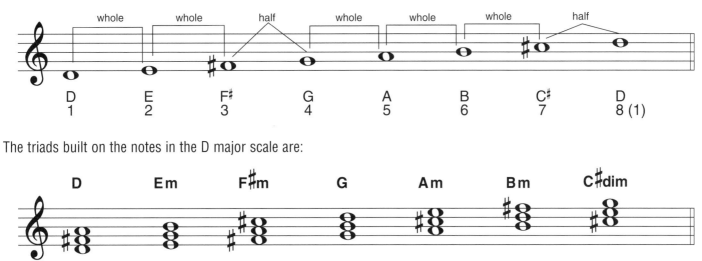

The triads built on the notes in the D major scale are:

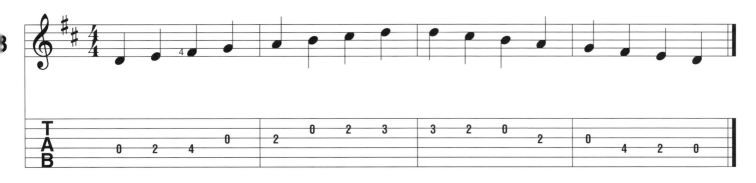

Practice the D major scale ascending and descending in first position. Remember: the key signature for D major is two sharps (F♯ and C♯).

RIFF IN D

The major scale step pattern can be applied to any root note to create any major scale. If you start on E, you will have an E major scale. If you start on F, you will have an F major scale. If you start on F♯, you will have an F♯ major scale, and so on.

SIXTEENTH NOTES

The **sixteenth note** has a solid oval head with a stem and either two flags or two beams. It lasts half as long as the eighth note.

The following chart shows the relationship of sixteenth notes to all the rhythmic values you have learned.

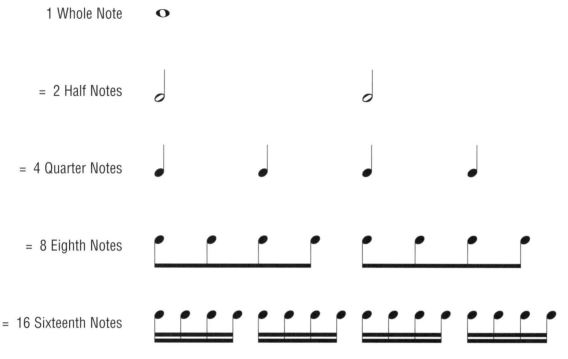

1 Whole Note

= 2 Half Notes

= 4 Quarter Notes

= 8 Eighth Notes

= 16 Sixteenth Notes

Since there are four sixteenth notes in one quarter note beat, count them by adding the syllables "e" and "a" (pronounced "uh"). The counting would be:

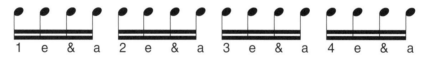

1 e & a 2 e & a 3 e & a 4 e & a

Practice the following sixteenth note exercises. Begin playing them slowly and accurately, then increase the tempo. Tap your foot on each beat of the measure.

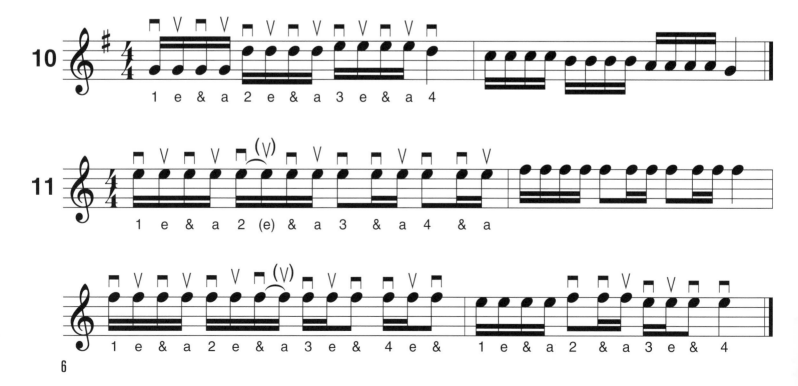

In $\frac{2}{4}$ time there are two beats per measure and the quarter note gets one beat.

ARKANSAS TRAVELER

Fiddle Tune

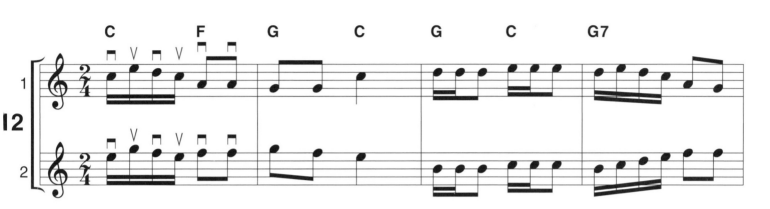

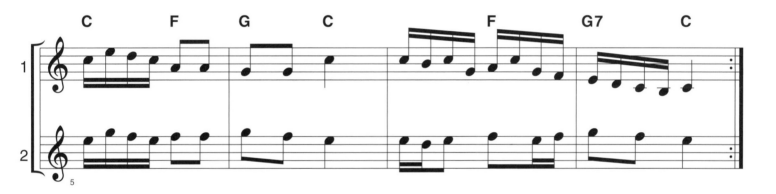

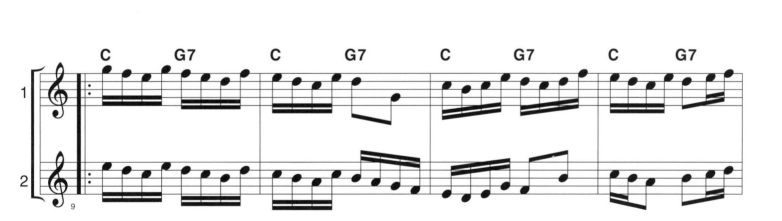

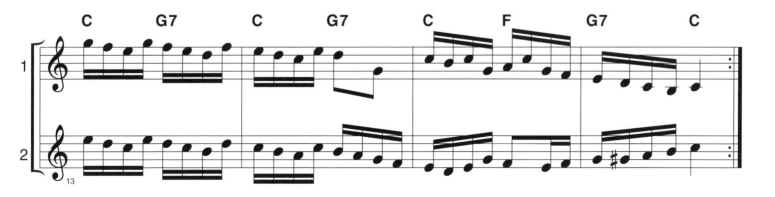

7

EXOTIC ROCK

FREEDOM ROCK

EINE KLEINE NACHTMUSIK
(A Little Night Music)

Mozart

DOTTED EIGHTH NOTES

Like the other dotted notes you've played, the dot after an eighth note increases the value of the note by one-half.

Since the dotted eighth receives only a part of a beat in $\frac{4}{4}$, $\frac{3}{4}$, or $\frac{2}{4}$ time, a sixteenth is added to it to complete the beat.

An easy way to learn a dotted eighth is to think of it as three tied sixteenth notes. This will help you play the rhythm more accurately. Practice the following exercise until you can play the subdivision of the beat easily.

TRAMP, TRAMP, TRAMP

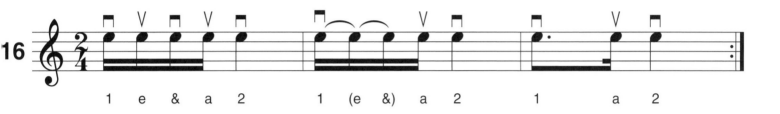

THE CHROMATIC SCALE

The **chromatic scale** is made up entirely of half-steps; therefore, it will use every available fret on the fretboard. If you play every fret on a given string from the open note to the twelfth fret, you will be playing a one-octave chromatic scale.

When playing the next example, hold down your fingers as you ascend on each string. Notice that sharps are used for the ascending scale while flats are used for the descent.

The diagram at the right shows all of the notes within the first twelve frets of the guitar fingerboard. Practicing the chromatic exercises below each day will greatly increase your finger dexterity and accuracy.

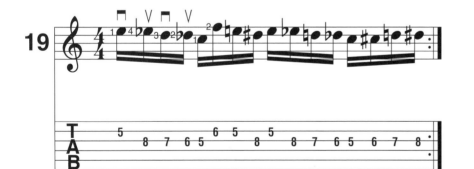

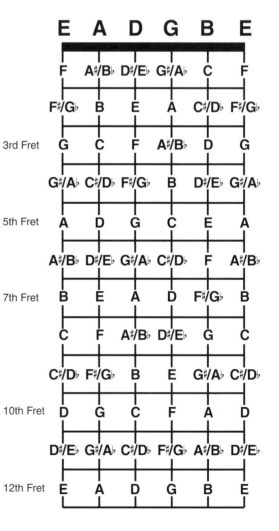

CUT TIME

Common Time C is another way of writing 4/4. Another way of writing 2/2 time (two beats per measure and the half note gets one beat) is ¢ **cut time**.

THE ENTERTAINER

Scott Joplin

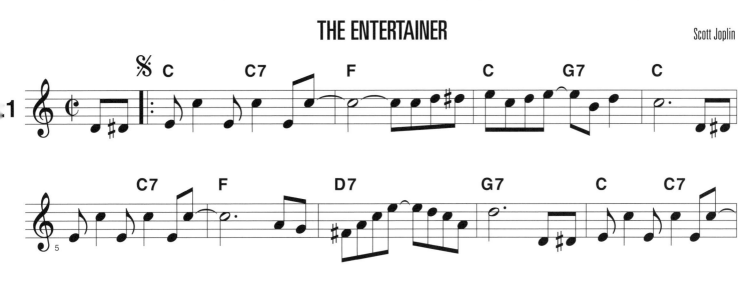

Play the next piece twice and gradually speed up.

IN THE HALL OF THE MOUNTAIN KING

E. Grieg

ESTUDIO

ST. LOUIS BLUES

W.C. Handy

BARRE CHORDS

Barre chords are chords in which two or more strings are depressed using the same finger. Most barre chords cover five or six strings and contain no open strings. The fingering shapes are movable and can be shifted up or down the neck to different positions to produce other chords of the same quality.

E-TYPE BARRE CHORD

One of the most useful movable barre chords is the one based on the open E chord. The root note of this E shape is on the sixth string. Therefore, this shape will be used to play major chords up and down the sixth string.

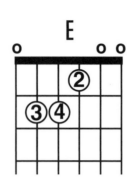

Follow these steps to form the E-type barre chord.

1. Play an open E chord, but use your 2nd, 3rd, and 4th fingers.

2. Slide this chord shape up one fret, and add your 1st finger across the 1st fret, forming a barre.

Strum all six strings to play your first barre chord. Make sure each string rings out clearly. Strike each note one at a time to test for clarity.

This particular barre chord is F major because its root is F on the sixth string. You can apply this same shape to any root note along the sixth string:

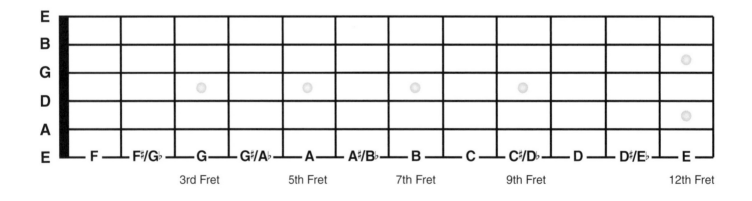

Now try the following barre chord exercise to get used to the feet of the movable shape.

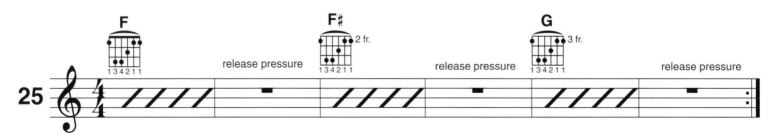

Once you are familiar with the basic feel and movement of the E-type major barre chord, it is easy to adapt this shape to form minor, seventh, and minor seventh barre chords.

If you subtract your 2nd finger from the major barre chord, you have a minor barre chord. If you subtract your 4th finger from the major barre chord, you have a seventh barre chord. If you subtract your 2nd and 4th fingers from the major barre chord, you have a minor seventh barre chord. Study the photos and diagrams below.

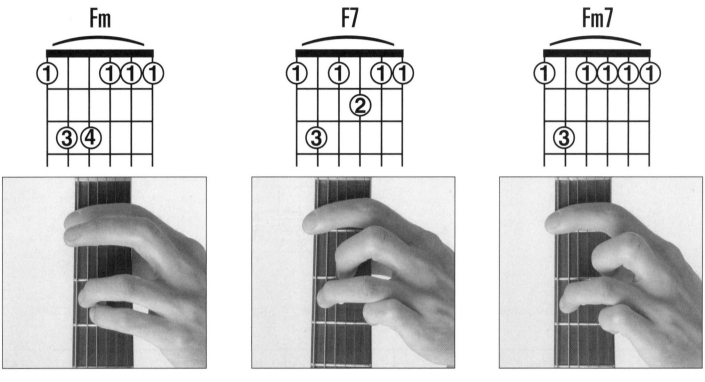

Try using these new barre chords in the examples below.

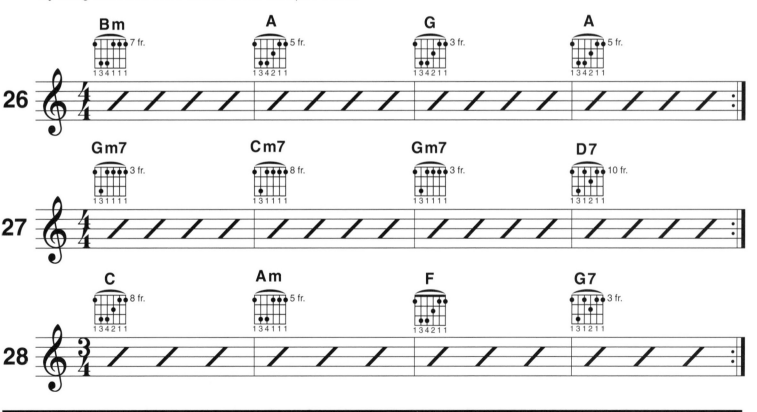

BARRE CHORD TIPS

Having difficulty at first in playing barre chords is normal. Here are some tips to help you:
- Instead of holding your first finger totally flat, rotate it a little onto its side nearest the thumb.
- Place your left thumb directly behind the first-finger barre for additional support.
- Move your elbow of your left arm in close to your body, even to the point that it's touching your body at the waist.

A-TYPE BARRE CHORD

The open A chord can also be converted to a barre chord. This shape will have its root on the fifth string. Follow these steps:

1. Play an open A chord, but use your 3rd finger to barre across strings 2-4.

2. Slide this chord shape up one fret, and add your 1st finger across the 1st fret, forming a barre.

The new B♭ barre chord can be tricky at first. If you are having trouble elevating the middle knuckle of your 3rd finger, you may want to avoid playing the first string (either by not striking it with the right hand or by muting it).

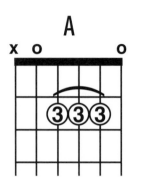

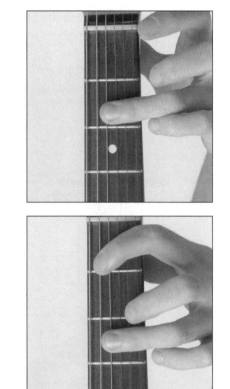

Practice the A-type major barre chord up and down the neck. Remember: the root of this shape lies along the fifth string.

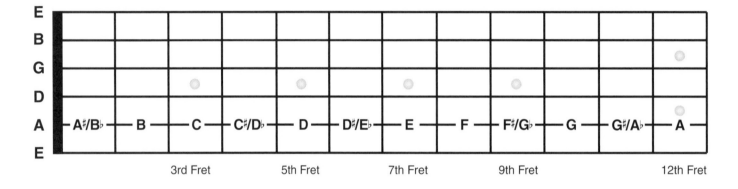

Now, use the major barre chord shape you just learned to play the following exercises.

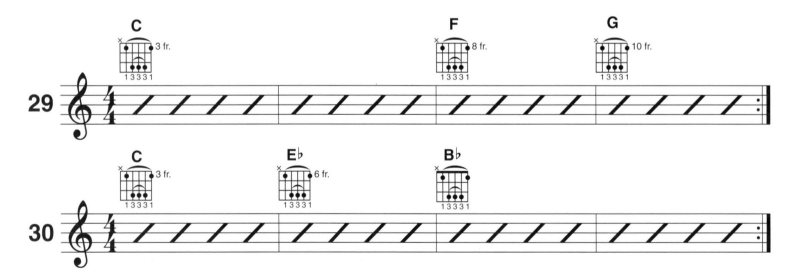

Playing barre chords on a electric guitar is easier than playing them on an acoustic guitar. This is because the **string gauges** (the thickness of the strings) are lighter on an electric guitar and the **action** (distance of the strings to the fretboard) is lower than on an acoustic.

The three barre chord shapes below are derived from the A-type major barre chord you just learned.

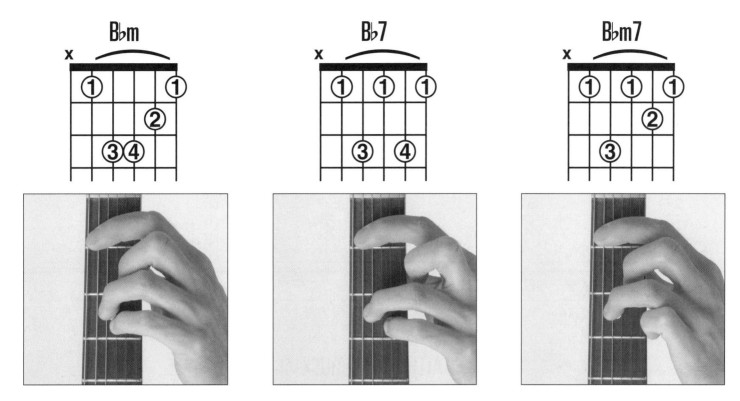

The following exercises combine the four A-type barre chords.

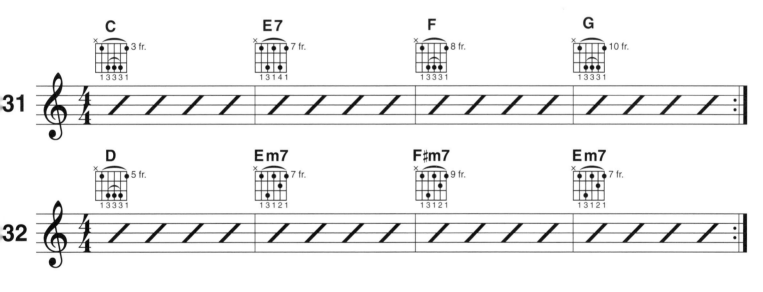

Sometimes you will see barre chords written in standard notation and tablature.

CLASSIC ROCK

Now try some some songs which use E-type and A-type barre chords.

SWINGIN'

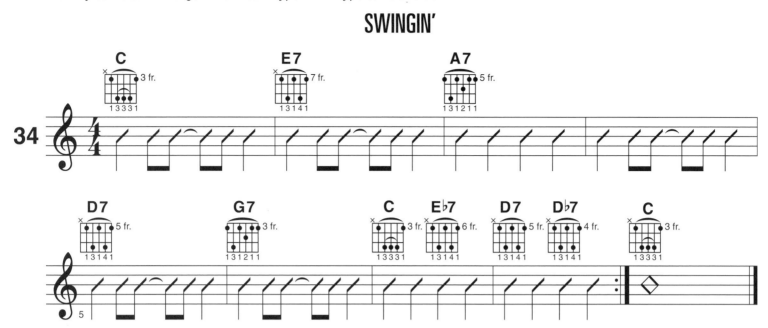

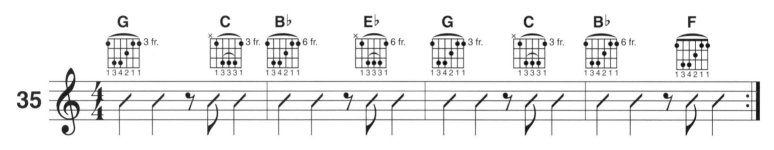

ALTERNATIVE ROCK

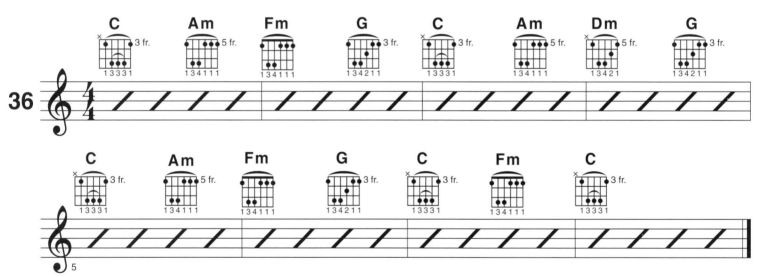

SLOW ROCK

In the next song, muted chords are indicated with an "X."

MINOR GROOVE

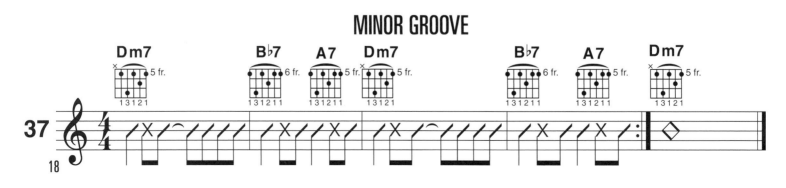

Some songs contain both barre chords and open chords.

JAZZY

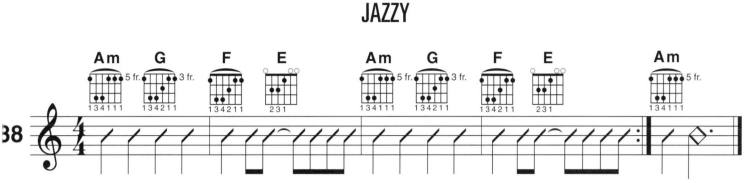

The next song introduces a new A-type barre chord: the major seventh chord. Also featured is a syncopated strum pattern that is common to Latin jazz.

BOSSA NOVA

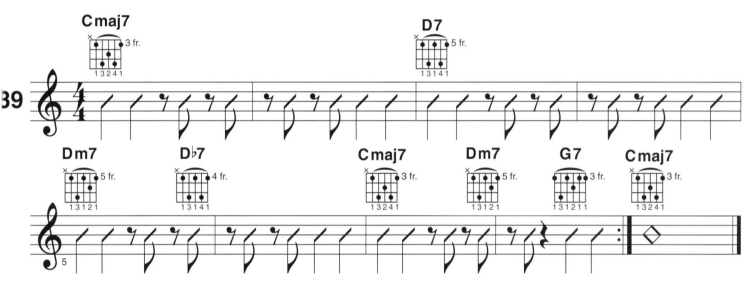

Now try mixing barre chords with single notes.

HARD ROCK

BARRE EXAM

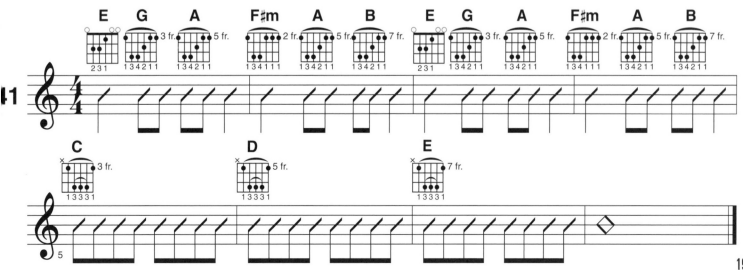

TRAVIS PICKING

Travis picking, named after country guitarist Merle Travis, is one of the most popular fingerstyle techniques. The style features two main characteristics:

- The thumb alternates between two bass strings, either on beats 1 and 3 or in steady quarter notes.
- The fingers pluck the higher strings, usually between the bass notes (on the off-beats).

The result is a driving, rhythmic feel that you can use for a variety of settings from ragtime to blues and beyond.

Practice each of the two main Travis picking patterns below. Notice the difference in the use of the thumb bass notes. Count the rhythms aloud as you play.

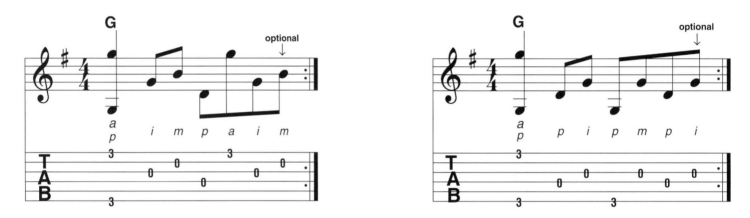

Now practice Travis picking on the following chord progressions. Start by playing one chord at a time; then gradually try moving from chord to chord. Optional bass notes are shown in parentheses.

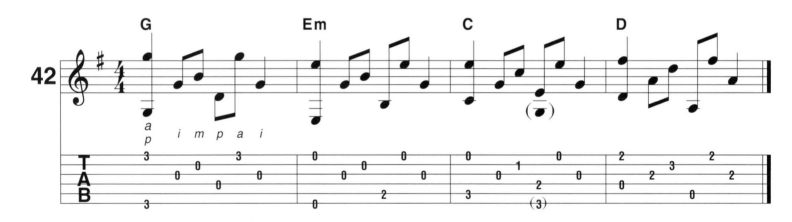

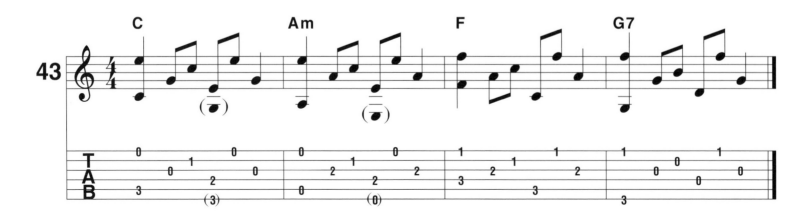

SOMETIMES I FEEL LIKE A MOTHERLESS CHILD

African American Traditional

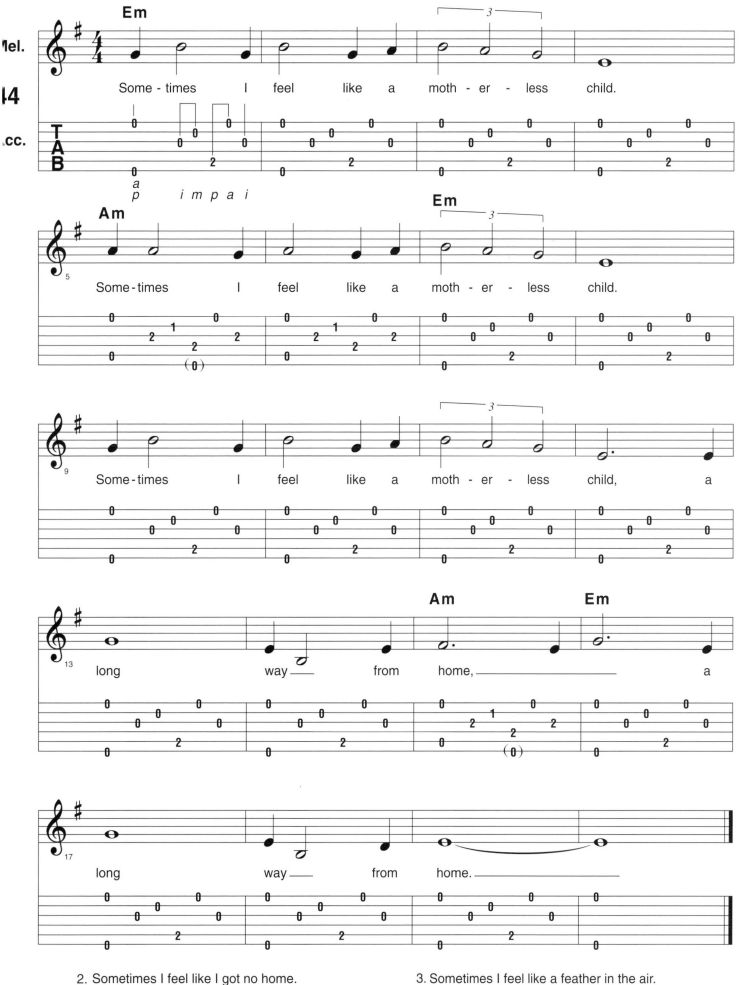

2. Sometimes I feel like I got no home.
   Sometimes I feel like I got no home.
   Sometimes I feel like I got no home,
   a long way from home, a long way from home.

3. Sometimes I feel like a feather in the air.
   Sometimes I feel like a feather in the air.
   Sometimes I feel like a feather in the air,
   a long way from home, a long way from home.

21

FREIGHT TRAIN

African American Traditional

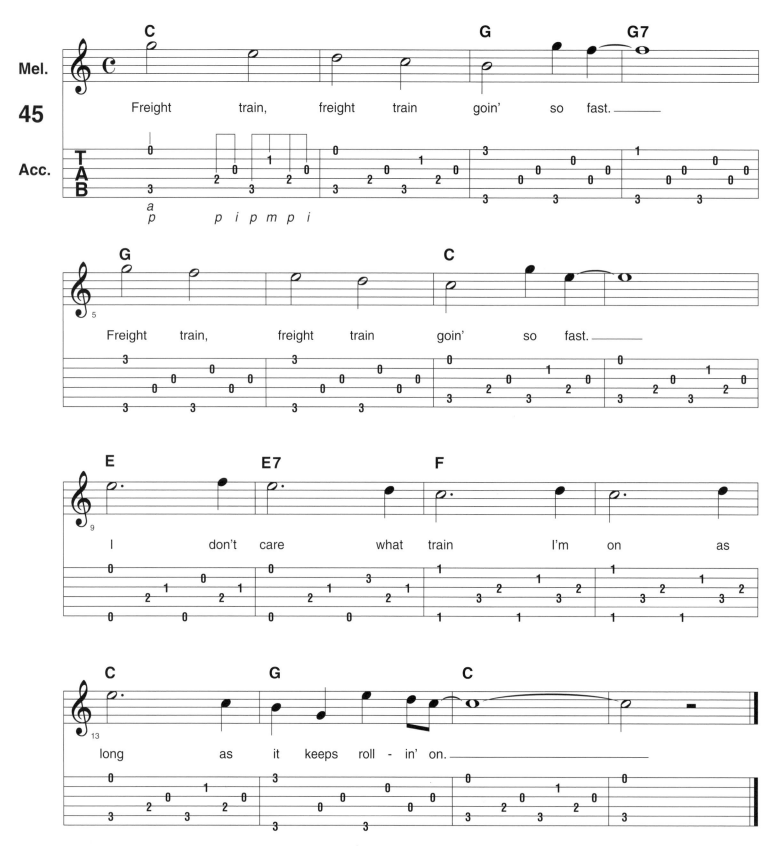

2. When I die, Lord, bury me deep
down at the end of old Chestnut Street.
So I can hear old Number Nine
as she comes rollin' down the line.

3. When I'm dead and in my grave,
no more good times will I crave.
Place a stone at my head and feet,
and tell them that I've gone to sleep.

DROP D TUNING

Alternate tunings are tunings other than the standard (low to high) E–A–D–G–B–E tuning. By using alternate tunings, you can achieve new, exciting sounds that are impossible to attain in standard tuning. Alternate tunings may also enable you to play licks or chords that are difficult to finger in standard tuning. Artists as diverse as Joni Mitchell, Robert Johnson, the Rolling Stones, and Nirvana make use of alternate tunings.

Drop D Tuning is the alternate tuning that is closest to standard tuning—you retune only the sixth string. To get into this tuning, lower (drop) your sixth string until it sounds an octave lower than your fourth string.

This tuning enables you to play a D (or Dm) chord with a low D as a root on the sixth string, giving you a full, rich sound.

POP/ROCK

An advantage of drop D tuning is that you can play low power chords on the bottom two strings as two-string barres, as shown in the next example.

GRUNGE

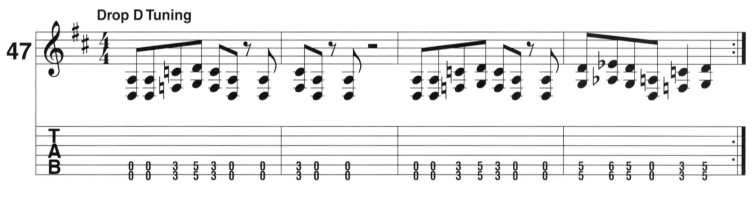

Finally, try mixing Travis Picking with drop D tuning.

FOLK/ROCK

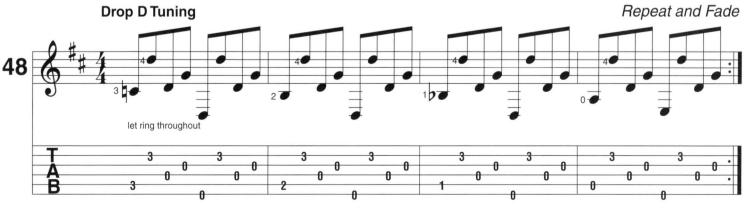

MOVABLE SCALES

You already know how to play scales in first position. To become a skillful soloist and proficient all-around guitarist, you must learn to play scales anywhere on the fingerboard.

The concept of movable scales is similar to that of power chords and barre chords. For each scale you will learn two movable patterns, one with its tonic on the sixth string and another with its tonic on the fifth string. By using these tonics as a point of reference, you can move the scales up and down the neck to accommodate any key. Simply match one of the tonics to its respective note on the fingerboard, and the rest of the pattern follows accordingly.

THE MAJOR SCALE

Study the following movable major scale patterns. Tonics are indicated with an open circle.

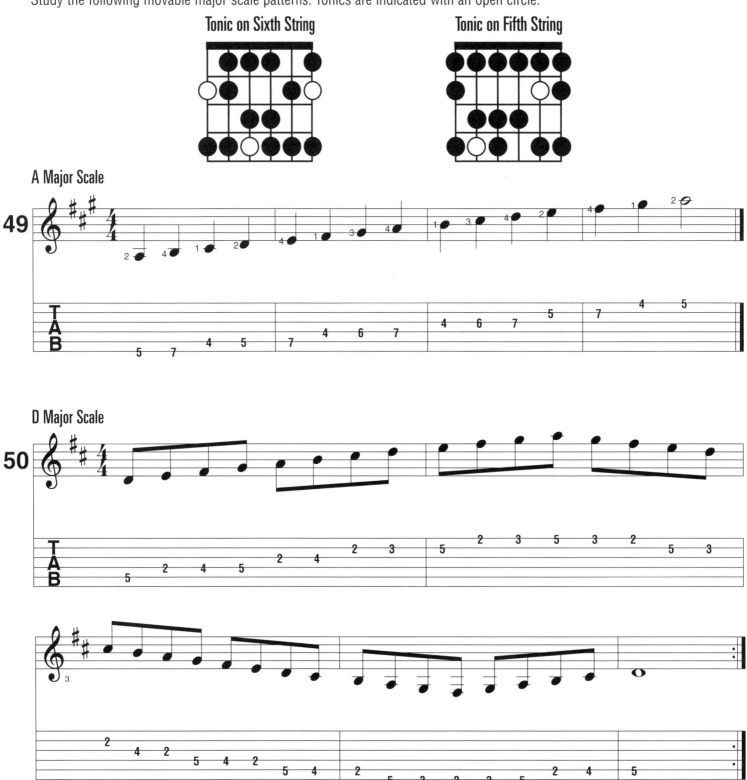

Tonic on Sixth String

Tonic on Fifth String

A Major Scale

D Major Scale

Use alternate picking as you practice the following major scale exercises.

G Major Scale Pattern

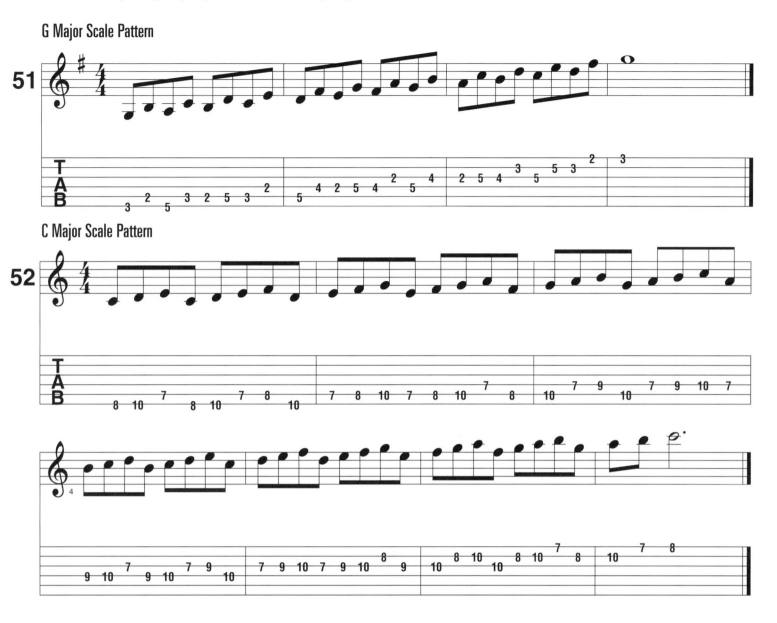

C Major Scale Pattern

MISS McLEOD'S REEL

Traditional

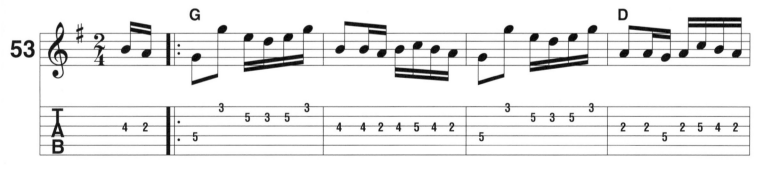

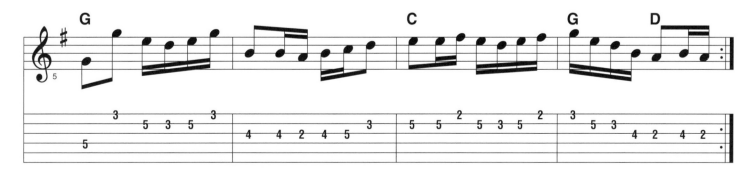

THE MINOR SCALE
Study the following movable minor scale patterns.

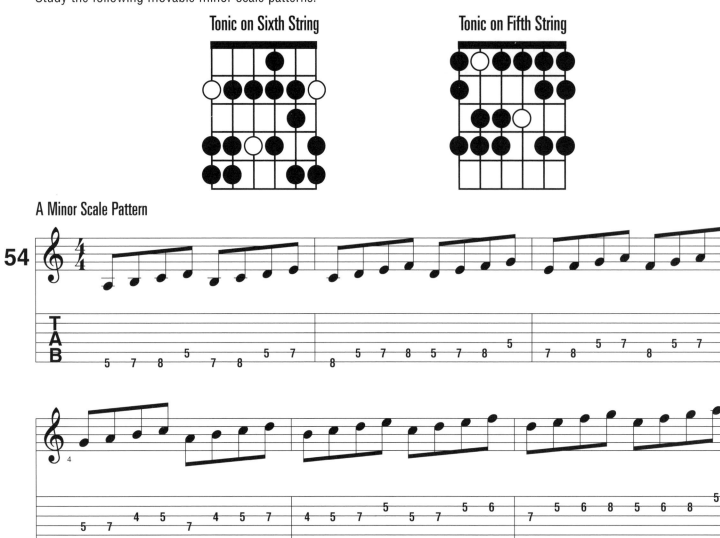

Tonic on Sixth String   **Tonic on Fifth String**

A Minor Scale Pattern

54

GOD REST YE MERRY GENTLEMEN
Christmas Carol

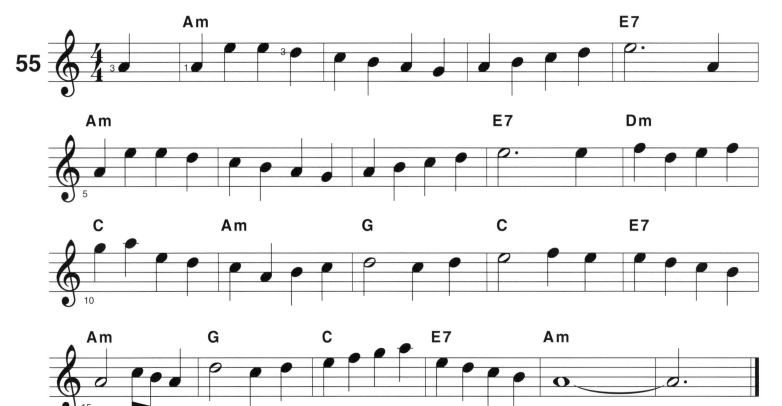

55

THE MINOR PENTATONIC SCALE
Study the following movable minor pentatonic scale patterns.

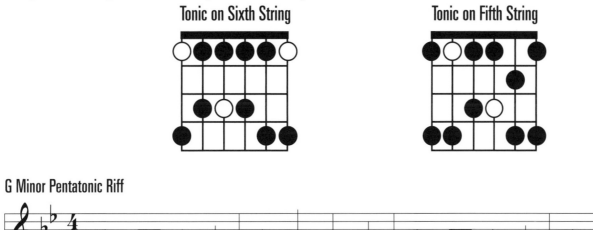

G Minor Pentatonic Riff

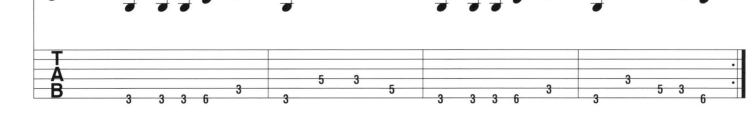

C Minor Pentatonic Lick

THE MAJOR PENTATONIC SCALE
Study the following movable major pentatonic scale patterns.

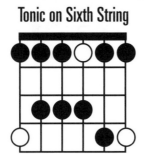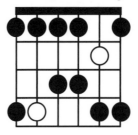

C Major Pentatonic Riff

The **fifth position** is very useful for playing songs, riffs, and licks in a higher position on the neck. Fingers 1, 2, 3, and 4 play in frets 5, 6, 7, and 8 as indicated in the diagram below.

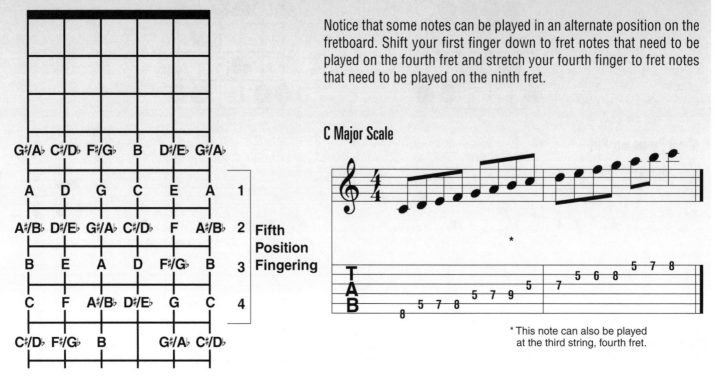

Notice that some notes can be played in an alternate position on the fretboard. Shift your first finger down to fret notes that need to be played on the fourth fret and stretch your fourth finger to fret notes that need to be played on the ninth fret.

C Major Scale

* This note can also be played at the third string, fourth fret.

DEEP RIVER

African-American Spiritual

BOUREE

J.S. Bach

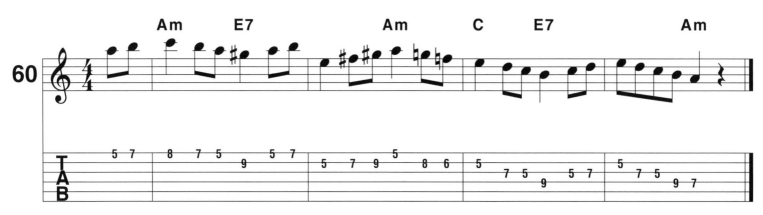

HEAVY ROCK

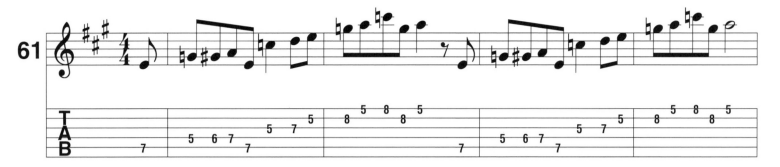

JAZZIN' THE BLUES

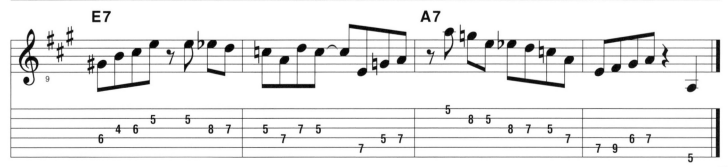

THE KEY OF F

The key signature for F has one flat. All Bs should be played one half step lower.

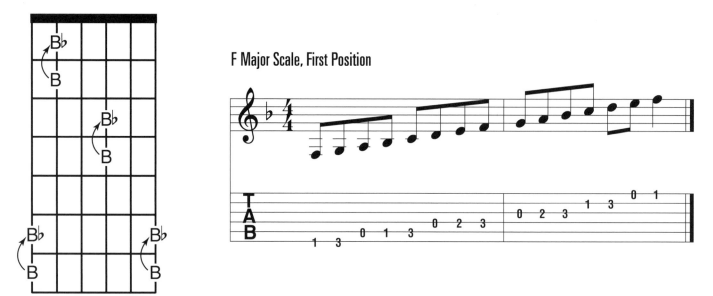

F Major Scale, First Position

Play the melody to "Sloop John B." in fifth position; then figure out how to play the chords to the song using the barre forms you learned on pages 14-19. You may also wish to try playing the Travis picking accompaniment from pages 20-22.

SLOOP JOHN B.

Caribbean

Refer to the "Circle of Fifths" on page 40 for more on keys.

COMPOUND TIME

Until now you have played time signatures in which the quarter note received one beat (e.g, $\frac{2}{4}$, $\frac{3}{4}$, $\frac{4}{4}$). The rhythmic pulse of these time signatures is divisible by two—four sixteenth notes equal two eighth notes, two eighth notes equal one quarter note, etc. This is called **simple time**. A time signature in which the rhythmic pulse is divisible by three is called **compound time**. The most common examples of compound time are $\frac{6}{8}$ and $\frac{12}{8}$.

$\frac{6}{8}$ TIME In $\frac{6}{8}$ time the bottom number tells you that the eighth note gets one beat and the top number tells you that there are six beats in one measure. All note and rest values are proportionate to the eighth note.

Eighth = 1 Beat   Quarter = 2 Beats   Dotted Quarter = 3 Beats

Practice playing "I Saw Three Ships" in fifth position. Be sure to follow the count carefully.

I SAW THREE SHIPS

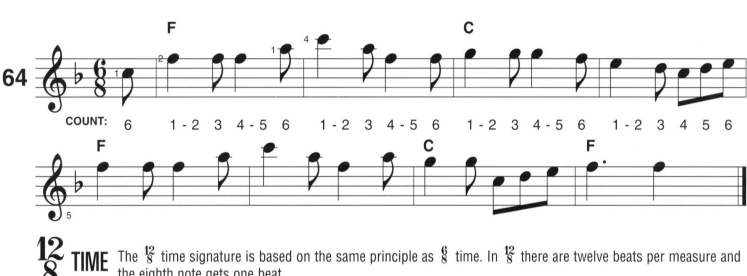

$\frac{12}{8}$ TIME The $\frac{12}{8}$ time signature is based on the same principle as $\frac{6}{8}$ time. In $\frac{12}{8}$ there are twelve beats per measure and the eighth note gets one beat.

SLOW BLUES

31

ARTICULATION

Articulation refers to how you play and connect notes on the guitar. If pitches and rhythms are what you play, articulation is how you play. **Slides**, **hammer-ons**, **pull-offs**, and **bends** all belong to a special category of articulations called **legato**. Legato techniques allow you to "slur" two or more notes together to create a smooth, flowing sound and help give your music flavor and expression.

THE SLIDE

The slide is played by following these steps:

- Depress the string with the left-hand finger.
- Pick the string with the right hand.
- Maintain pressure as you move your left-hand finger up or down the fretboard to the second position shown. (The second note is not picked.)

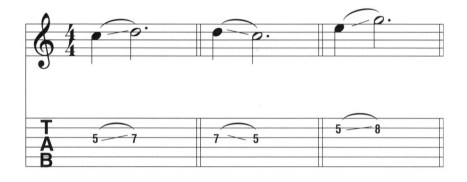

BOUNCY BLUES

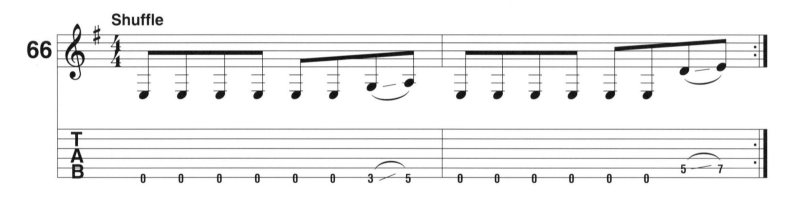

POWER CHORD SLIDES

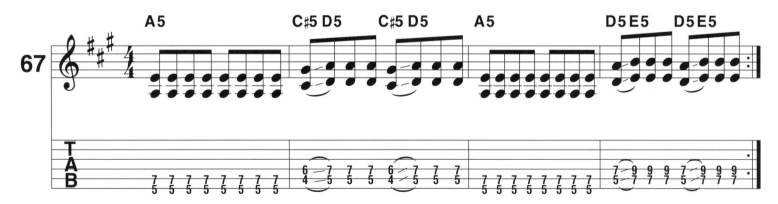

THE HAMMER-ON

The **hammer-on** is named for the action of the left-hand fingers on the fretboard. To play the hammer-on follow these steps:

- Depress the string with the left-hand finger.
- Pick the string with the right hand.
- Maintain pressure as you quickly press down onto the fret of the second (higher) note on the same string, using the initial attack to carry the tone.

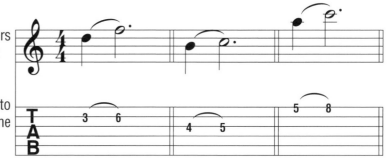

FOLK PATTERN

ROCK 'N' HAMMER

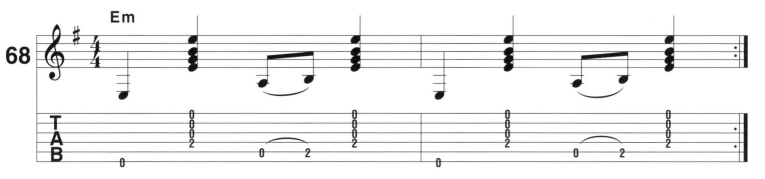

ACOUSTIC ROCK

BOOGIE BLUES

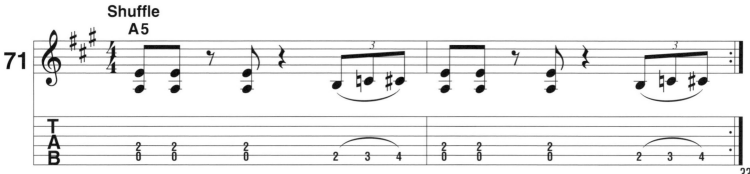

THE PULL-OFF

The **pull-off** is the opposite of the hammer-on. To play the pull-off follow these steps:

- Depress the string with the left-hand finger.
- Pick the string with the right hand.
- Maintain pressure as you pull the left-hand finger toward the palm of your hand to sound the note behind it on the same string, using the initial attack to carry the tone.

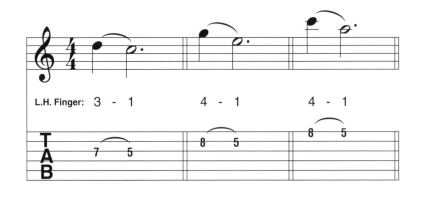

POWER PULL

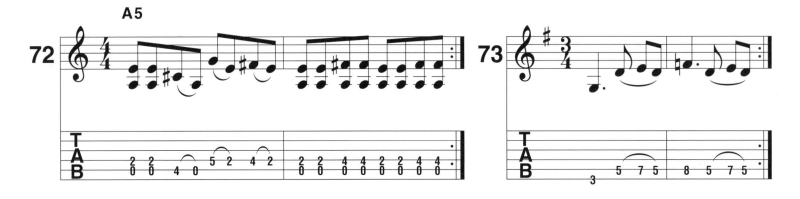

BLUES WALTZ

Hammer-ons, pull-offs, and slides are all used in the next example.

BLUEGRASS RUN

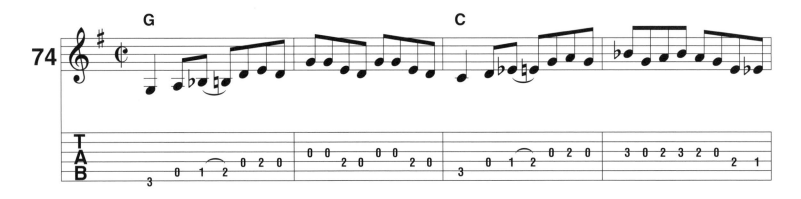

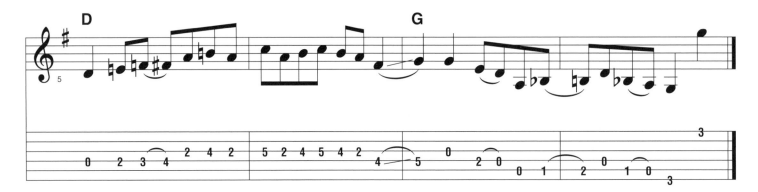

THE STRING BEND

The **string bend** produces the vocal-like sound of blues, rock, and pop guitar. To bend a string follow these steps:

- Depress the string with the left-hand 3rd finger.
- Maintain pressure as you push the string upward or pull it downward.
- Use your first and second fingers for additional support.

Bends are indicated in music by a pointed slur in standard notation and an arrow in tablature. Bending strings works best on steel-string guitars and is done most easily on the first three strings.

To the right are some characteristic bends:

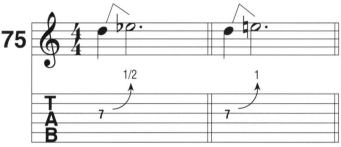

ROCK LICK

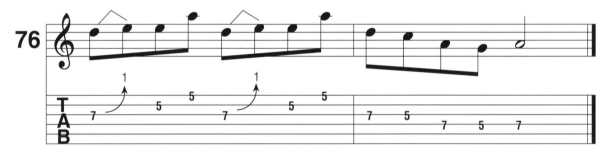

The next example contains a bend and release. Maintain pressure as you lower the bend back to its original pitch.

SWAMPY BLUES

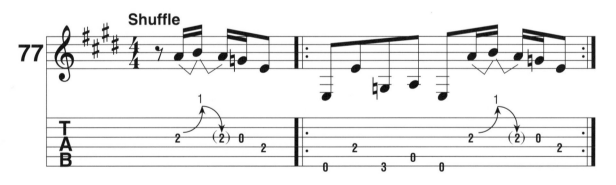

Now try bending two strings at the same time.

DOUBLE-STOP BEND

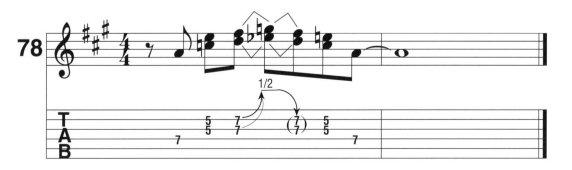

JAM SESSION

Now it is time to use the chords and scales you know to make some of your own music. This section provides ten chord progressions found in various music styles. You can either follow the chord symbols and strum along, or use the suggested scales to practice improvising. Listen to the recording and copy the solo licks; then try creating your own solos. If you don't have the recording, take turns playing rhythm and leads with friends or record your own rhythm tracks and play lead over them.

POP/ROCK BALLAD
Suggested scales: G major and G major pentatonic

FUNK
Suggested scale: A minor pentatonic

SMOOTH JAZZ
Suggested scales: C major and C major pentatonic

LATIN ROCK
Suggested scales: D minor and D minor pentatonic

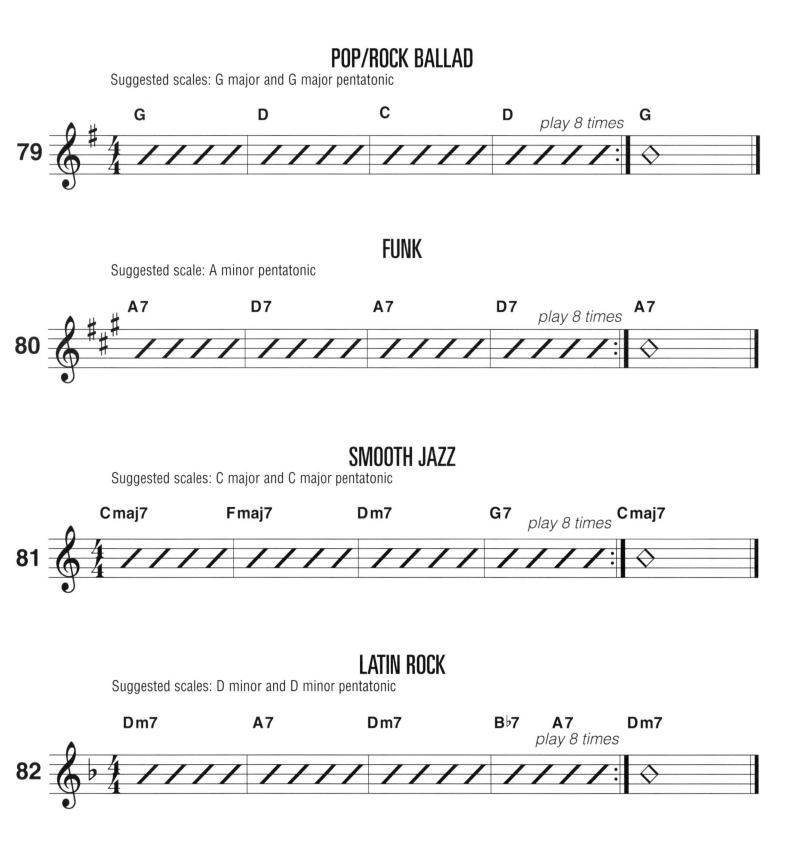

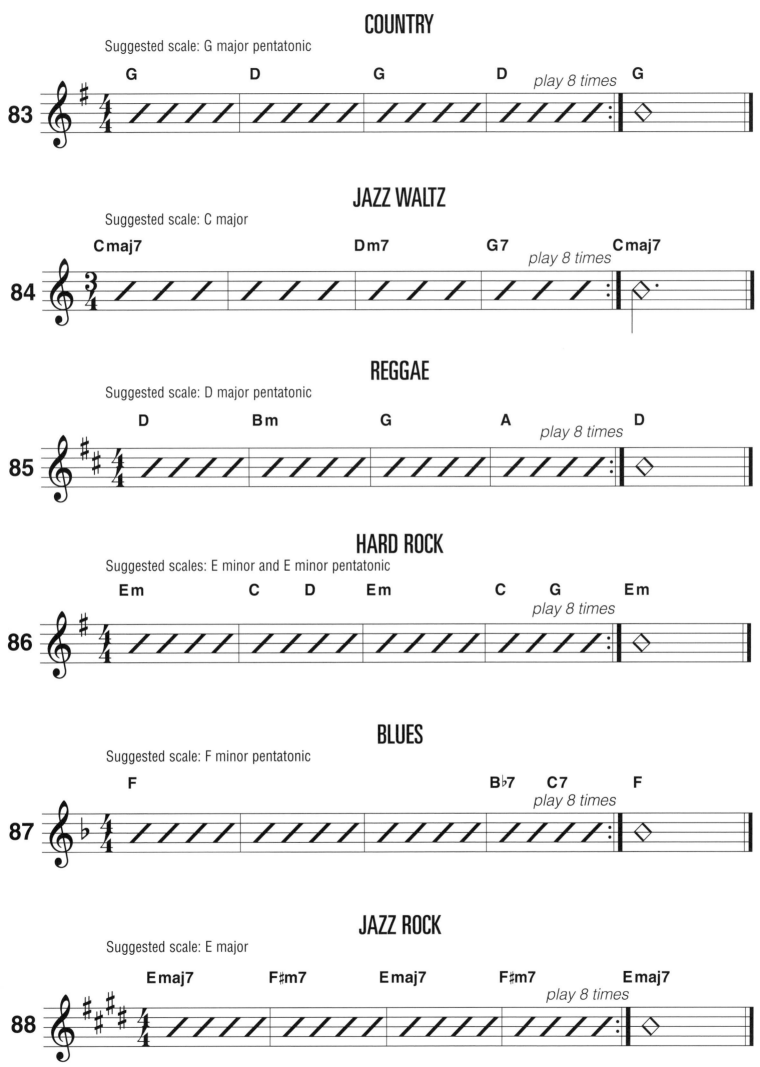

GRAND FINALE

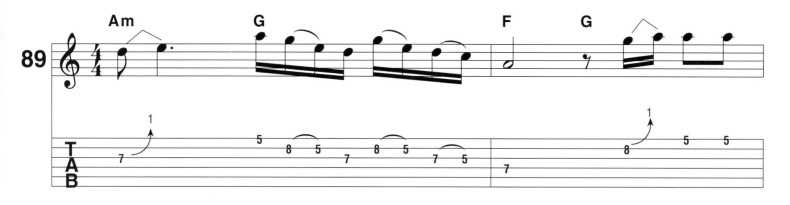

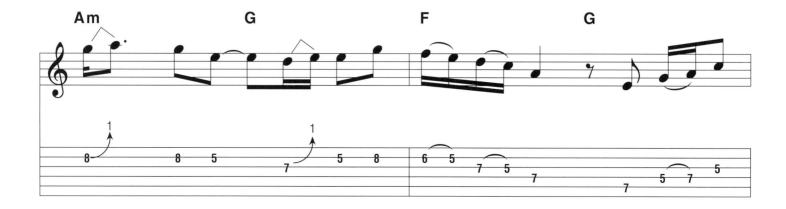

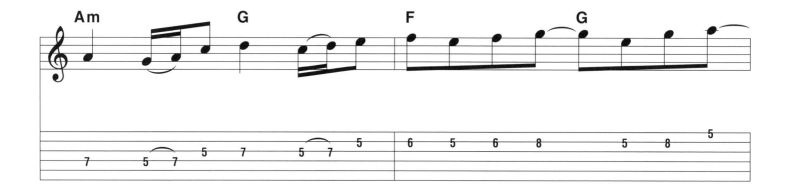

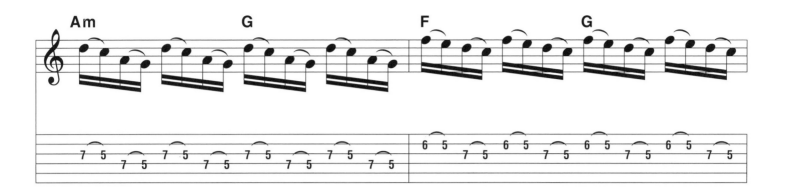

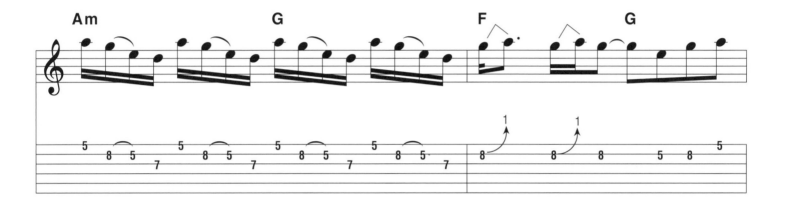

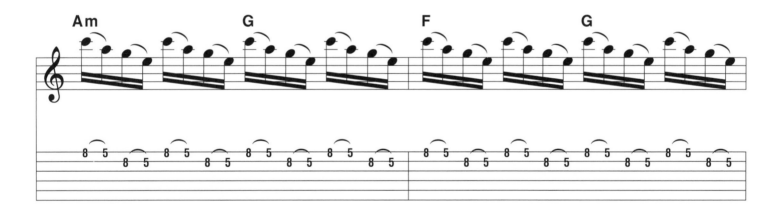

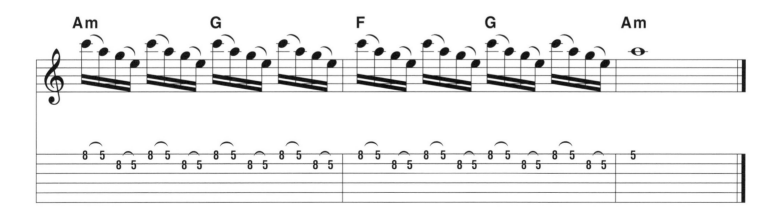

REFERENCE SECTION

CIRCLE OF FIFTHS

The **circle of fifths** is a useful tool if you want to know what chords are common within a key. Major keys line the outside of the circle; their relative minors line the inside.

Right now, the box is highlighting chords that belong to both C major and its relative A minor. To find the chords for another key, just mentally rotate the box.

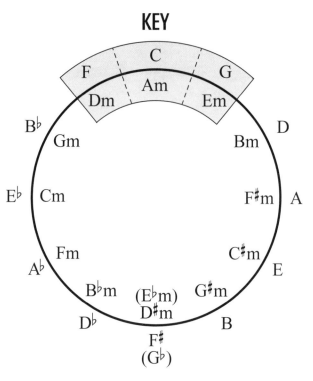

THREE-NOTE CHORD FORMS

These movable three-note shapes are easy to play and commonly used in pop, funk, and reggae styles. Pay attention to the root in each voicing; it tells you what chord you are playing.

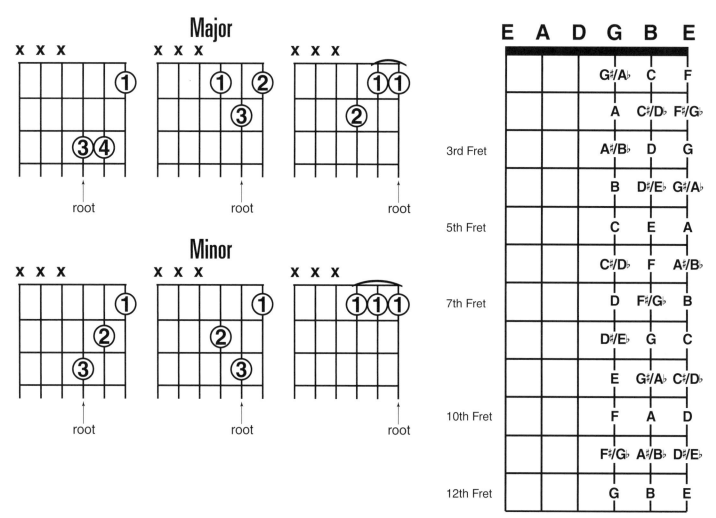

MISCELLANEOUS CHORDS

Below are some less common open chords which you have not learned up to this point.

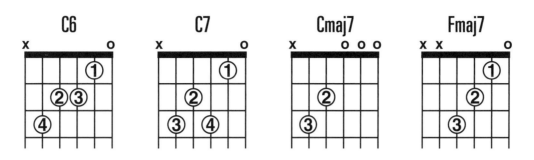

In **sus chords**, you replace the third of a chord with the fourth, as in sus4 (pronounced "suss-four") or sometimes with the second, as in sus2. The resulting sound is incomplete or unresolved but creates an interesting sound that is neither major nor minor.

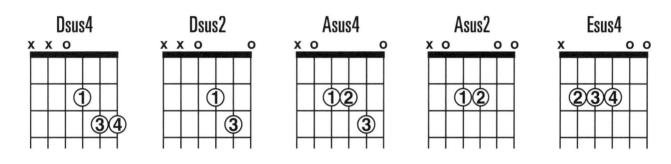

An **add chord** is simply a basic chord (such as a major chord) to which you add an extra note. If you take a C chord and add a D note to it, for example, you have a Cadd2 chord (with notes C–D–E–G). This chord is different from Csus2, which has no E.

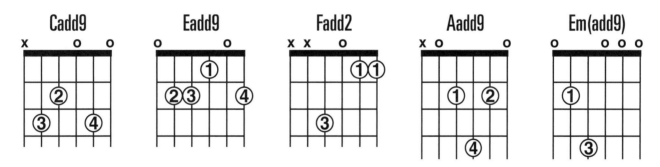

Slash chords are colorful, interesting chords that add spice and flavor to all styles of music. A slash chord is, simply, a chord with a slash (/) in its name, as in G/B (pronounced "G over B"). To the left of the slash is the chord itself; to the right of the slash is the bass note for that chord.

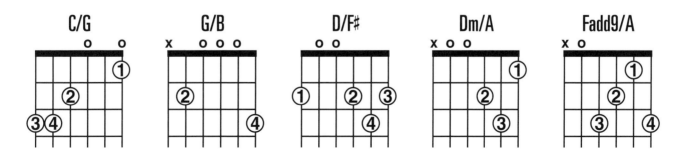

CHORD CONSTRUCTION

All chords are constructed using intervals. An **interval** is the distance between any two notes. Though there are many types of intervals, there are only five categories: major, minor, perfect, augmented, and diminished. Interestingly, the major scale contains only major and perfect intervals:

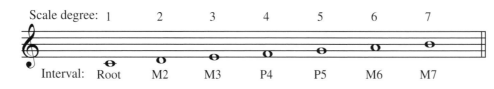

The major scale also happens to be a great starting point from which to construct chords. For example, if we start at the root (C) and add the interval of a major third (E) and a perfect fifth (G), we have constructed a C major chord.

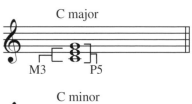

In order to construct a chord other than a major chord, at least one of the major or perfect intervals needs to be altered. For example, take the C major chord you just constructed, and lower the third degree (E) one half step. We now have a C minor chord: C-E♭-G. By lowering the major third by one half step, we create a new interval called a **minor** third.

We can further alter the chord by flatting the perfect fifth (G). The chord is now a Cdim: C-E♭-G♭. The G♭ represents a **diminished** fifth interval.

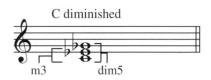

This leads us to a basic rule of thumb to help remember interval alterations:

A major interval lowered one half step is a minor interval.

A perfect interval lowered one half step is a diminished interval.

A perfect interval raised one half step is an augmented interval.

Half steps and whole steps are the building blocks of intervals; they determine an interval's quality—major, minor, etc. On the guitar, a half step is just the distance from one fret to the next. A whole step is equal to two half steps, or two frets.

Notice that we assigned a numerical value to each note in the major scale, as well as labeling the intervals. These numerical values, termed **scale degrees**, allow us to "generically" construct chords, regardless of key. For example, a major chord consists of the root (1), major third (3), and perfect fifth (5). Substitute any major scale for the C major scale above, select scale degrees 1, 3, and 5, and you will have a major chord for the scale you selected.

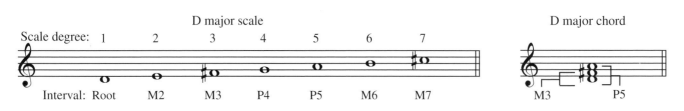

The chart below is a construction summary of 44 chord types (based on the key of C only) using the scale degree method:

CHORD TYPE	FORMULA	NOTES	CHORD NAME
major	1-3-5	C-E-G	C
fifth (power chord)	1-5	C-G	C5
suspended fourth	1-4-5	C-F-G	Csus4
suspended second	1-2-5	C-D-G	Csus2
added ninth	1-3-5-9	C-E-G-D	Cadd9
sixth	1-3-5-6	C-E-G-A	C6
sixth, added ninth	1-3-5-6-9	C-E-G-A-D	C6/9
major seventh	1-3-5-7	C-E-G-B	Cmaj7
major ninth	1-3-5-7-9	C-E-G-B-D	Cmaj9
major seventh, sharp eleventh	1-3-5-7-#11	C-E-G-B-F#	Cmaj7#11
major thirteenth	1-3-5-7-9-13	C-E-G-B-D-A	Cmaj13
minor	1-♭3-5	C-E♭-G	Cm
minor, added ninth	1-♭3-5-9	C-E♭-G-D	Cm(add9)
minor sixth	1-♭3-5-6	C-E♭-G-A	Cm6
minor, flat sixth	1-♭3-5-♭6	C-E♭-G-A♭	Cm♭6
minor sixth, added ninth	1-♭3-5-6-9	C-Eb-G-A-D	Cm6/9
minor seventh	1-♭3-5-♭7	C-E♭-G-B♭	Cm7
minor seventh, flat fifth	1-♭3-♭5-♭7	C-E♭-G♭-B♭	Cm7♭5
minor, major seventh	1-♭3-5-7	C-E♭-G-B	Cm(maj7)
minor ninth	1-♭3-5-♭7-9	C-E♭-G-B♭-D	Cm9
minor ninth, flat fifth	1-♭3-♭5-♭7-9	C-E♭-G♭-B♭-D	Cm9♭5
minor ninth, major seventh	1-♭3-5-7-9	C-E♭-G-B-D	Cm9(maj7)
minor eleventh	1-♭3-5-♭7-9-11	C-E♭-G-B♭-D-F	Cm11
minor thirteenth	1-♭3-5-♭7-9-11-13	C-E♭-G-B♭-D-F-A	Cm13
dominant seventh	1-3-5-♭7	C-E-G-B♭	C7
seventh, suspended fourth	1-4-5-♭7	C-F-G-B♭	C7sus4
seventh, flat fifth	1-3-♭5-♭7	C-E-G♭-B♭	C7♭5
ninth	1-3-5-♭7-9	C-E-G-B♭-D	C9
ninth, suspended fourth	1-4-5-♭7-9	C-F-G-B♭-D	C9sus4
ninth, flat fifth	1-3-♭5-♭7-9	C-E-G♭-B♭-D	C9♭5
seventh, flat ninth	1-3-5-♭7-♭9	C-E-G-B♭-D♭	C7♭9
seventh, sharp ninth	1-3-5-♭7-#9	C-E-G-B♭-D#	C7#9
seventh, flat fifth, sharp ninth	1-3-♭5-♭7-#9	C-E-G♭-B♭-D#	C7♭5(#9)
eleventh	1-5-♭7-9-11	C-G-B♭-D-F	C11
seventh, sharp eleventh	1-3-5-♭7-#11	C-E-G-B♭-F#	C7#11
thirteenth	1-3-5-♭7-9-13	C-E-G-B♭-D-A	C13
thirteenth, suspended fourth	1-4-5-♭7-9-13	C-F-G-B♭-D-A	C13sus4
augmented	1-3-#5	C-E-G#	Caug
seventh, sharp fifth	1-3-#5-♭7	C-E-G#-B♭	Caug7
ninth, sharp fifth	1-3-#5-♭7-9	C-E-G#-B♭-D	Caug9
seventh, sharp fifth, flat ninth	1-3-#5-♭7-♭9	C-E-G#-B♭-D♭	Caug7♭9
seventh, sharp fifth, sharp ninth	1-3-#5-♭7-#9	C-E-G#-B♭-D#	Caug7#9
diminished	1-♭3-♭5	C-E♭-G♭	Cdim
diminished seventh	1-♭3-♭5-♭♭7	C-E♭-G♭-B♭♭	Cdim7

Triads

The most basic chords are called triads. A **triad** is a chord that is made up of only three notes. For example, a simple G major chord is a triad consisting of the notes G, B, and D. There are several types of triads, including major, minor, diminished, augmented, and suspended. All of these chords are constructed by simply altering the relationships between the root note and the intervals.

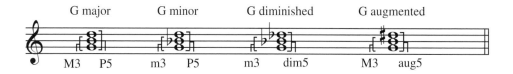

Sevenths

To create more interesting harmony, you can take the familiar triad and add another interval: the seventh. **Seventh chords** are comprised of four notes: the three notes of the triad plus a major or minor seventh interval. For example, if you use the G major triad (G-B-D) and add a major seventh interval (F#), the Gmaj7 chord is formed. Likewise, if you substitute the minor seventh interval (F) for the F#, you have a new seventh chord, the G7. This is also known as a dominant seventh chord, popularly used in blues and jazz music. As with the triads, seventh chords come in many types, including major, minor, diminished, augmented, suspended, and others.

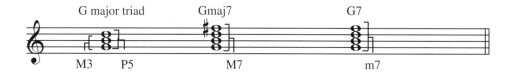

Extended chords

Extended chords are those that include notes beyond the seventh scale degree. These chords have a rich, complex harmony that is very common in jazz music. These include ninths, elevenths, and thirteenth chords. For example, if you take a Gmaj7 chord and add a major ninth interval (A), you get a Gmaj9 chord (G-B-D-F#-A). You can then add an additional interval, a major thirteenth (E), to form a Gmaj13 chord (G-B-D-F#-A-E). Note that the interval of a major eleventh is omitted. This is because the major eleventh sonically conflicts with the major third interval, creating a dissonance.

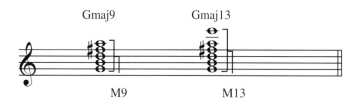

By the way, you may have noticed that these last two chords, Gmaj9 and Gmaj13, contain five and six notes, respectively; however, you only have four fingers in the left hand! Since the use of a barre chord or open-string chord is not always possible, you often need to choose the four notes of the chord that are most important to play. Below are two examples to demonstrate these chord "trimmings."

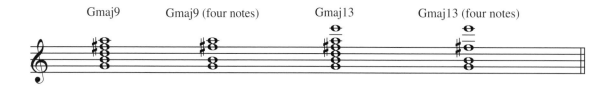

Generally speaking, the root, third, and seventh are the most crucial notes to include in an extended chord, along with the uppermost extension (ninth, thirteenth, etc.).

Inversions & Voicings

This brings us to our last topic. Though a typical chord might consist of only three or four notes—a C triad, for example, consists of just a root, third, and fifth; a G7 chord consists of a root, third, fifth, and seventh—these notes do not necessarily have to appear in that same order, from bottom to top, in the actual chords you play. Inversions are produced when you rearrange the notes of a chord:

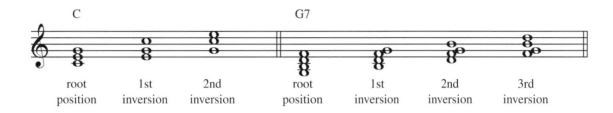

Practically speaking, on the guitar, notes of a chord are often inverted (rearranged), doubled (used more than once), and even omitted to create different voicings. Each voicing is unique and yet similar—kind of like different shades of the same color.

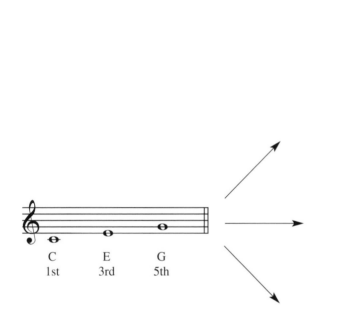
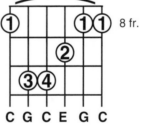
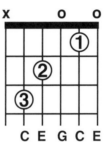
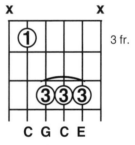
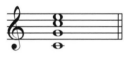

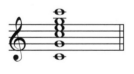

Study the construction of the chords below.

A major scale: A–B–C#–D–E–F#–G#

D major scale: D–E–F#–G–A–B–C#

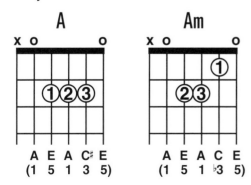
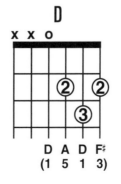
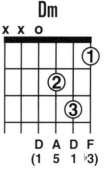
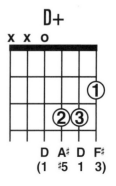

GEAR

Following are some basic guidelines to consider when choosing electric guitar equipment.

Guitars

There are three general types of electric guitars: solidbody, hollowbody, and semi-hollowbody. The **solidbody guitar** is associated most with rock, blues, country, and soul. The most popular models include the Fender Stratocaster, Gibson Les Paul, Paul Reed Smith, Fender Telecaster, Gibson SG, and Ibanez RG. The solidbody guitar is typically heavier than others. Its density permits more sustain and makes it better suited for high-volume playing. The **hollowbody guitar** is the choice of most jazz guitarists. It is distinguished by its arched top and back, f-shaped sound holes, and deep sides. The most popular models include the Gibson ES-175, Gibson L-5, Gibson Super 400, Epiphone Emperor, Heritage Eagle, Guild Manhattan, and various makes by D'Angelico, D'Aquisto, and Benedetto. The tone of the hollowbody guitar is more subdued than that of the solidbody, and its basic design makes it better suited for low to mid volume playing. The **semi-hollowbody guitar** has a thin, semi-hollow body with a solid wooden strip in the center. The most popular models include the Gibson ES-355, Gibson ES-345, Guild Starfire IV, Heritage H-535, and Epiphone Sheraton. It is most commonly used by blues, jazz-rock, and rock guitarists, and is known for providing the best of both worlds in terms of tone: more crisp than a hollowbody and more mellow than a solidbody.

The playability of various electric guitars is subjective. In trying to decide on a prospective guitar, consider the neck radius, scale length, neck material (rosewood, maple, ebony), string gauge, and fret size.

Amps

There are two general types of amps: tube and solid-state. **Tube amps** are so-named because they are powered by and get their tonal characteristics from vacuum tubes. They produce a warm, smooth clean tone and, when the volume is turned up, a natural distortion. They are favored by most blues, jazz, country, and roots-rock guitarists. **Solid-state amps** use transistors for power and tone. They are typically more reliable and versatile than tube amps and have come a long way in recent years in terms of being able to produce a warm tone. In the late 1990s, digital modeling technology has enabled solid-state amps to access an assortment of classic tube amp tones and a myriad of effects. Solid-state amps are preferred by most modern rock guitarists, but are also widely used for playing all musical styles.

Effects

Effects are devices that plug in between your guitar and amp and enable you to alter your signal in a variety of ways. They are available as individual units, called **foot pedals**, or as an all-in-one box, called a **multi-effects processor**. Following is a list of the most popular effects:

Distortion	Simulates the sound of a guitar signal driven too hard for the amp; the effect can produce anything from a bright, fuzzy tone to a thick, dirty tone.
Chorus	Simulates the sound of two guitars playing at once; the effect can produce anything from a lush, chiming sound to a warbled, fluttering sound.
Delay or Echo	Simulates the repetition of sound; the effect can add depth to your tone by producing anything from a short, "slap back" delay to a longer, ambient looping sound.
Reverb	Simulates the natural echo produced in various rooms; the effect can produce anything from a washy, distant-sounding ambiance to a live, airy sound.
Wah-Wah Pedal	Produces a sweeping, vocal-like tone by rocking the treble back and forth.

Pickups

There are two general types of pickups: humbucking (double-coil) and single-coil. **Humbucking pickups** produce a dark, mellow sound when playing with a clean tone and a thick, heavy tone when playing with a distorted tone. **Single-coil pickups** produce a glassy, percussive sound when playing with a clean tone and an aggressive, biting tone when playing with a distorted tone.

DEFINITIONS FOR SPECIAL GUITAR NOTATION

HALF-STEP BEND: Strike the note and bend up 1/2 step.

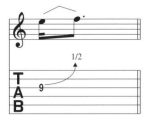

WHOLE-STEP BEND: Strike the note and bend up one step.

GRACE NOTE BEND: Strike the note and immediately bend up as indicated.

SLIGHT (MICROTONE) BEND: Strike the note and bend up 1/4 step.

BEND AND RELEASE: Strike the note and bend up as indicated, then release back to the original note. Only the first note is struck.

PRE-BEND: Bend the note as indicated, then strike it.

PRE-BEND AND RELEASE: Bend the note as indicated. Strike it and release the bend back to the original note.

UNISON BEND: Strike the two notes simultaneously and bend the lower note up to the pitch of the higher.

VIBRATO: The string is vibrated by rapidly bending and releasing the note with the fretting hand.

WIDE VIBRATO: The pitch is varied to a greater degree by vibrating with the fretting hand.

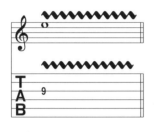

HAMMER-ON: Strike the first (lower) note with one finger, then sound the higher note (on the same string) with another finger by fretting it without picking.

PULL-OFF: Place both fingers on the notes to be sounded. Strike the first note and without picking, pull the finger off to sound the second (lower) note.

LEGATO SLIDE: Strike the first note and then slide the same fret-hand finger up or down to the second note. The second note is not struck.

SHIFT SLIDE: Same as legato slide, except the second note is struck.

TRILL: Very rapidly alternate between the notes indicated by continuously hammering on and pulling off.

TAPPING: Hammer ("tap") the fret indicated with the pick-hand index or middle finger and pull off to the note fretted by the fret hand.

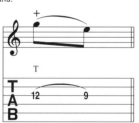

NATURAL HARMONIC: Strike the note while the fret-hand lightly touches the string directly over the fret indicated.

Harm.

PINCH HARMONIC: The note is fretted normally and a harmonic is produced by adding the edge of the thumb or the tip of the index finger of the pick hand to the normal pick attack.

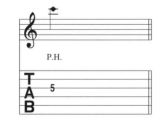

P.H.

ARPEGGIATE: Play the notes of the chord indicated by quickly rolling them from bottom to top.

PICK SCRAPE: The edge of the pick is rubbed down (or up) the string, producing a scratchy sound.

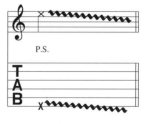

P.S.

MUFFLED STRINGS: A percussive sound is produced by laying the fret hand across the string(s) without depressing, and striking them with the pick hand.

PALM MUTING: The note is partially muted by the pick hand lightly touching the string(s) just before the bridge.

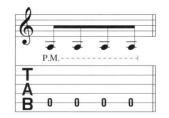

P.M.

RAKE: Drag the pick across the strings indicated with a single motion.

rake- - - -

TREMOLO PICKING: The note is picked as rapidly and continuously as possible.

HAL LEONARD GUITAR METHOD